J
976.8   **Thompson, Kathleen**
T   **Tennessee**

TENNESSEE

A Turner Educational Services, Inc. book. Based on the Portrait
of America television series created by R.E. (Ted) Turner.

Library of Congress Number: 85-12173

1234567890   908988878685

Library of Congress Cataloging in Publication Data

Thompson, Kathleen.
  Tennessee.

  (Portrait of America)
  "A Turner book."
  Summary: Discusses the history, economy, culture,
and future of Tennessee. Also includes a state
chronology, pertinent statistics, and maps.
    1. Tennessee—Juvenile literature. [1. Tennessee]
I. Title. II. Series: Thompson, Kathleen. Portrait of
America.
F436.3.T46   1985   976.8   85-12173
ISBN 0-86514-444-3 (lib. bdg.)
ISBN 0-86514-519-9 (softcover)

Cover Photo: State of Tennessee Photographic Service

★ ★ ★ ★ ★
Portrait of AMERICA

TENNESSEE

Kathleen Thompson

Photographs from Portrait of America programs
courtesy of Turner Program Services, Inc.

A TURNER BOOK
RAINTREE PUBLISHERS

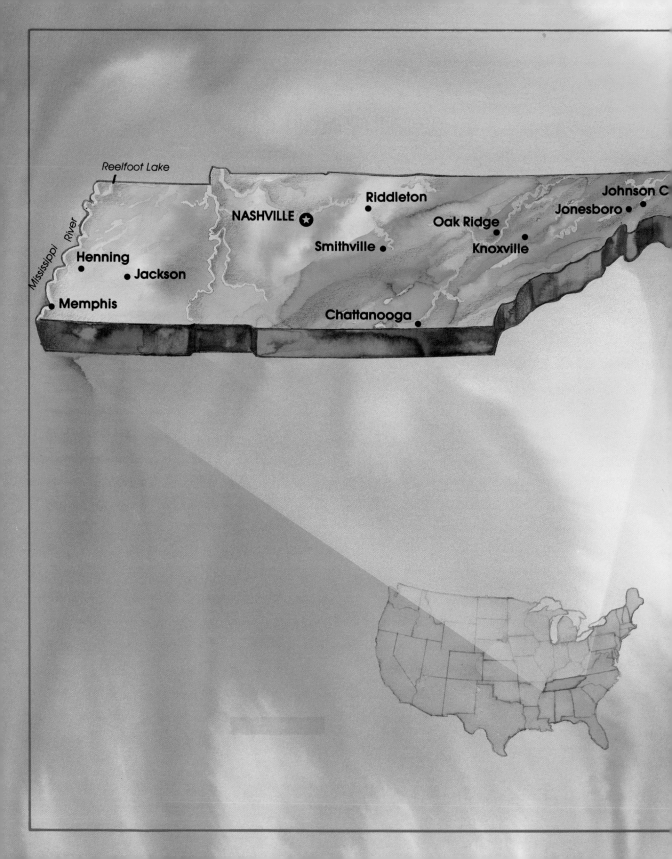

CONTENTS

Introduction

Tennessee, the Volunteer State.

"The two words home *and* Tennessee *hyphenate for me. I really have traveled the world now, pretty much. I've been so blessed to do that. But nowhere, I don't care where I am, I am never very far from Henning, Tennessee."*

Tennessee: music, mountains, the Battle of Shiloh, pioneers, plastics.

"We work together. If we get in trouble, we can call in neighbors. They'll come in and help. It's a friendly, wholesome, good place to live."

"Never did think anything about leaving. I made my living here. I've just got to piddle around here the rest of my days."

To some people, Tennessee is Nashville, the home of country music. To some, it's Memphis, home of the blues. To some people, Tennessee is the Great Smoky Mountains and the Blue Ridge Valley. And to others it's a bustling industrial state.

In its early days, Tennessee was a place for pioneers. It still is.

Roan Mountain in the Appalachians.

Land of the Pioneers

Before Europeans came, most of Tennessee was part of vast hunting grounds for the Cherokee and the Chickasaw Indians. Among the tall trees and rugged mountains, hunters killed game needed to feed their families and then returned to small towns scattered around the edges.

It was a startlingly beautiful place, rich in wildlife. Many tribes hunted here. No one broke the ground for farms or cut the trees to build homes. It was a wild country.

Spanish explorers were the first Europeans to enter the land. Hernando de Soto passed through in 1540, raiding Indian towns on his way.

More than a hundred years passed before English and French traders arrived, in the same year. Their arrival marked the beginning of a struggle between these two great powers for the Indians' land. Each country tried to gain the cooperation of the Cherokees in defeating the other. The French, who were always more successful at making friends with the Indians, won that battle but lost the war. In 1763, the British claims were recognized by the French.

Those claims were not, however, recognized by the Cherokees. They traded with the British as they had traded with the French. But they kept trying to preserve their hunting grounds. When white hunters came into the forests, they were warned by the Indians. Often, they were escorted out of the region—without their furs. Daniel Boone was more than once treated to this friendly but firm method.

But the land was too tempting. The hunters would go back to their families and friends with glowing reports of the beauty of the rich forests and rivers. The British had outlawed any settlement west of the Appalachians, but soon the pioneers were coming in anyway.

The first permanent settlement was probably the one founded in 1769 by William Bean. He came from Virginia and settled on the Watauga River. Others came from North Carolina.

These early settlers were mostly English, Scotch-Irish, and German. Over the years, their isolation in the hills meant that a lot of their culture and even their language would remain very little changed. Even today, you can hear traces of old English speech patterns and traditional English, Scotch, and Irish tunes, and see dances that hark back to seventeenth-century Britain.

By 1772, there were four areas of settlement in northeastern Tennessee. Only one of them was on land that belonged, legally, to whites. The British superintendent of Indian affairs ordered the other three communities to move, but they refused. Finally, they agreed to lease the land from the Cherokees. They also set up their own government, called the Watauga Association.

At this time, the Tennessee

This nineteenth-century painting depicts Daniel Boone leading settlers through the Cumberland Gap.

area actually belonged to North Carolina. But the pioneers were separated from the rest of the colony by mountains. They never really functioned as part of the North Carolina colony.

When the Revolutionary War broke out in 1775, the people living in Tennessee supported the colonists. During the Revolution, a group called the Transylvania Company met with the Cherokees and bought a piece of land that included parts of Tennessee and Kentucky. At the same time, the Watauga Association changed their lease into a purchase.

The Transylvania Company sent Daniel Boone into the wilderness he had once illegally hunted. He blazed a trail from Virginia, across the mountains at Cumberland Gap, and into western Tennessee. It was the famous Wilderness Road and it brought new settlers into the area.

The spot chosen by the Transylvania Company as headquarters for its settlement was on the Cumberland River. They sent James Robertson to build Fort Nashborough, now called Nashville. An agreement called the Cumberland Compact set up a temporary government in the area.

In 1784, North Carolina turned over its Tennessee territory to the federal government. The people living there organized a new state, which they named Franklin, in honor of Benjamin Franklin. Then North Carolina decided it wanted the area back.

But the Franklinites did not give up their new state. For four years they fought the Indians who said the land belonged to them and they argued with North Carolina, which said the land belonged to it. In 1789, North Carolina gained control of the region again. Then, it gave the area back to the federal government. Congress organized the whole area we now call Tennessee into the Territory of the United States South of the River Ohio.

The Chickasaw still owned nearly all of western Tennessee. And the Cherokee held two large areas within the region. When Tennessee became a state in 1796, the people demanded that the federal government get rid of the Indians. Treaties were made with both the Cherokee and the Chickasaw for parts of the land. But the Cherokee had, by this time, adopted many of the European ways. They had towns and farms. Many wore European clothes and had adopted European names. The Cherokee scholar Sequoyah had developed an alphabet and there were newspapers.

The United States government had to force families off their farms and businessmen out of their stores in order to clear the land for white settlement. In 1838, the Cherokee were forcibly moved to Oklahoma.

At the right is one of the rooms of a reconstruction of Fort Nashborough. In the background is a reproduction of part of the Cumberland Compact.

... shall be determined ...
... may be ... the following manner ...
... the free ... of this Country over the ...
... Years shall immediately or as soon as may ...
... and choose twelve Conscientious and ...
Persons ... of the different Stations, That is ...
... from Nashborough three from Gaspers two ...
... Ashers one, ... River one ...
... one, Eatons two Fort ... one ...
... which said persons or a majority of them, after being ...
by the solemnity of an Oath to do equal and impartial ...
... between all contending parties, according to ...
... them shall in Judgment ... and ...
... the Regulations of the ...
... shall be competent Judge ...
... hearing the Allegations ...
... as to the facts ...
... as to the truth of the ...
... decide the controversies, an ...
... intitled to an entry for such ...
said Determination or ...
... conclusive, against the ...
... against whom such ...
... the Entry ... shall ...
... Book accordingly and the Entry ...

Metro Board of Parks and Recreation, Nashville, TN

In 1796, when it became a state, there were about 77,000 people living in Tennessee. Some of them were slaves, owned by farmers in west and middle Tennessee. Some were free blacks. Under the constitution of the new state, those free blacks had the right to vote. They kept that right until 1834, when a new constitution was approved.

There were three men from Tennessee in the early years of the state who went on to become presidents of the United States. Andrew Jackson was the first. He gained national fame during the War of 1812 when he led U.S. forces at the Battle of New Orleans.

That war was a popular one in Tennessee. Large numbers of men volunteered to fight. That happened again during the Mexi-can War, and Tennessee got its nickname as the Volunteer State.

Andrew Jackson was elected President of the United States in 1828. James K. Polk, his close friend, was elected in 1845.

The third man, Andrew Johnson, began his political career as a state senator. He fought for the rights of the poor. He had held slaves and did not oppose slavery, but he did oppose states withdrawing from the Union. He served as Tennessee's representative to the U.S. Congress and as governor of Tennessee. When Abraham Lincoln was elected president in 1861, Andrew Johnson was U.S. senator from Tennessee.

Johnson tried very hard to keep his state in the Union. And he had some support from the people of his state. But when the Civil War broke out, more than two-thirds of the people voted to withdraw from the Union. Andrew Johnson was the only Southern senator who refused to secede with his state.

On the left-hand page are three Tennesseeans who became president of the United States: Andrew Jackson (top, left), Andrew Johnson (top, right), and James K. Polk (bottom).

15

In this photograph Confederate and Union soldiers posed together under one flag after the Civil War.

Tennessee was caught in the middle during the Civil War in more ways than one. For one thing, there were sympathizers for both sides in the state. For another, Tennessee's location made it one of the two leading battlegrounds in the war. More than 400 battles or skirmishes were fought in this one state. They included the famous battles at Shiloh and Chickamauga.

After the war, Andrew Johnson was elected to the vice-presidency under Abraham Lincoln. On April 14, 1865, Lincoln was assassinated. Johnson was inaugurated the next day.

On July 24, 1866, Tennessee, the last state to leave the Union, became the first state to be readmitted. As a result, it escaped the harsh program of Reconstruction that was imposed on the other ten states of the Confederacy.

But the time following the Civil War was nonetheless a terrible one in Tennessee. The fighting had left much of the state in ruin. Thousands of people had no homes. Thousands had been killed in the war.

A group called the Radical Republicans took over the state government. For the second time in the state's history, blacks were given the right to vote. And that right was taken away from many who had been involved in the Confederacy. In 1869, the Radical Republicans were voted out of office in an election that was surrounded by Ku Klux Klan activity. Blacks

At the right is William G. Browlow, a Radical Republican, who was governor of Tennessee from 1865 to 1869.

were threatened with death if they exercised their newly won right to vote. Many black sympathizers saw the burning cross in their front yards.

Recovery from the war was slow. And the second half of the nineteenth century was marked by conflict. In the 1870s and 1880s, farmers who were suffering terrible economic problems organized the Grange and the Farmers Alliance and agitated for relief. Coal miners went on strike against working conditions in the mines, and convicts from the state's prisons were brought in to break the strikes. In 1891 and 1892 there was the so-called "Coal Miners War." There were yellow fever epidemics. In 1878, Memphis lost 5,200 of its 19,600 residents to yellow fever.

In the meantime, manufacturing and mining were growing in the state. They helped to make up for the jobs lost as the farms went under.

In 1925, the world was suddenly watching Dayton, Tennessee. When a high school teacher named John Scopes broke the law of Tennessee by teaching evolution in his school, two of the country's greatest lawyers were brought in to try the case. William Jennings Bryan was the prosecuting attorney and Clarence Darrow, the defense attorney.

Scopes lost in the courts and was fined $100. But he and the forces who opposed fundamentalist religious control of the schools won in the national press. The "monkey trial" gave Tennessee a reputation it would spend years living down. The anti-evolution law was repealed in 1967.

In this photograph of the Scopes trial, William Jennings Bryan (standing) is making a speech to the jury.

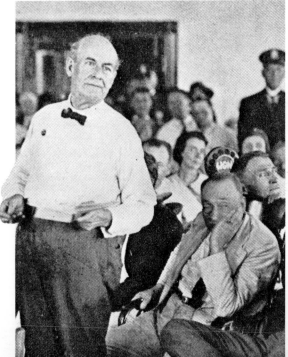

The Douglas Dam, one of the many built under the Tennessee Valley Authority.

During the Great Depression, the federal government formed the Tennessee Valley Authority. The TVA built dams and roads and offered jobs to the unemployed. After World War II, the activities of the TVA continued. Soon, there was cheap electrical power and plenty of water in most parts of the state. This brought in new industry. It also brought in lots of tourists. The economy of Tennessee grew.

More and more, Tennessee was becoming a manufacturing state. More and more, people were moving from farms into the cities. In 1962, the Supreme Court of the United States ruled that federal courts have the right to order states to make representation in their legislatures fairer. In 1965, under court order, Tennessee reorganized its legislative districts to make representation more nearly equal according to population. This gave the cities more control.

At the same time, battles were being fought to desegregrate public schools and public accommodations. In 1968, Doctor Martin Luther King, Jr., went to Memphis to lead protests for striking garbage workers. On April 14, he was assassinated. The days that followed were a terrible time for Tennessee and the rest of the nation.

Today, Tennessee is a state where the pioneer past is always peeking through into the industrial present. Its mountains, forests, and rivers seem as lovely now as when they were the Cherokee hunting ground. And the people still show a strong spirit of independence, ingenuity, and frontier spirit.

A Place to Remember

"This little gadget here on the floor is a baby rocker that came from Blind Maggie Graves up in Big Valley. She could sit here and rock the cradle and peel apples or break beans or quilt or whatever she wanted to do . . . . For years, nobody could figure out what it was."

Gadgets and guitars and old shoes. John Rice Irwin has them all at his seventy-five-acre Appalachian museum. Here is the evidence of a way of life. Here the great grandchildren of the pioneers are reminded of how their ancestors lived in the early days of Tennessee.

"They had to make their own clothing, their own shoes. They had to be their own blacksmiths and make their own wagons and everything that had to be done, they had to do themselves. They couldn't go to the supermarket and buy it. In Appalachia, it was a little more that way because you had people who were so isolated you could not have the specialization that you had in some other sections of the country."

John Rice Irwin's family had been in this region for two hundred years. The first things to go into his collection were given to him by his grandfather. Now, there are more than two hundred thousand items. Some of them are old, some not so old. Things haven't changed completely in Appalachia, even after the Tennessee Valley Authority with its dams brought electrical power and paved roads.

Against the background of his property is John Rice Irwin.

Museum of Appalachia

John Rice Irwin is shown below with a banjo made from a ham can. At the right is part of Irwin's property, and above is a reconstruction of the interior of Daniel Boone's cabin, which is part of Irwin's museum.

Portrait of America

"This, I guess, maybe indicates that the ingenuity and the 'make-do' has not all disappeared from the mountains, because my old friend Dow Pugh from down in Montgomery, Tennessee, made this about twenty-eight years ago. And he saw this ham can—$2.98 on it—and he puts a neck on it and has a real nice-playing banjo."

To John Rice Irwin, this museum is a matter of pride. Like other groups around the country, the people of Appalachia have a need to understand and be proud of their heritage.

"There's so many people that Tennessee has produced that were what I think were great people. People that I would consider to be great you never heard of because they lived on a little farm and spent their life there. I feel sort of an obligation to try to tell their grandsons and their great-grandsons and so forth how it was. And if they see some of the things—the pair of shoes that Uncle Camel wore for twenty-four years and how he patched them and so forth—they might get a little bit of appreciation of him and the contributions he made."

Museum of Appalachia

Rooted in Tennessee

"And I remember there was an old man. I don't know his name and I doubt if either of you do. On Saturday mornings, like now, an old man would come every morning and sit on an upturned Coke bottle—I mean a Coke carton, wooden carton—right about there. And he would just sit and bend over like that. And a little crowd would start gathering. And he would stay there and the crowd would get a little bit bigger."

Alex Haley, author of the best-selling book *Roots*, remembers his childhood. He remembers summers in Henning, Tennessee, and an old man downtown on Saturday morning.

"Around 10:30 in the morning, his hand would go out for the first time, and he caught a fly."

That was Man Brady, a friend reminds him.

"Was that Man Brady? And what fantastic reflexes. And he would, every Saturday, get crowds to watch him snatch a fly."

Before television, people found lots of ways to entertain themselves in a small town like Henning. And lots of ways to dream. Railroads were always good for a dream or two.

On the right-hand page, against the background of his boyhood home in Henning, is Alex Haley. Above is the railroad that runs through Henning.

"These train tracks. Nothing about this town, Henning, Tennessee, is more integral to its history, to my image of it, my memory of it, because these tracks were the link with the outside world."

The outside world. Who knew what was waiting there? Who knew what possibilities lay beyond the horizon? Some of the trains went north, the land of opportunity for a young black child in Tennessee.

"And we would watch—little boys; little girls would have to stand over there on the side by the fences, but little boys could come right up near the tracks—and then when the trains would leave we would all run up and get right behind it, safely behind it, and we would run in the center of the track, like here, for maybe a mile as the train chuffed, chuffed, picked up speed, and went on its way to Memphis or back this way to New Orleans or Chicago. And we would, as we ran, dream that one day we would grow up and be able to get enough money to buy us a ticket to go north and do good."

Melissa Brandon

Portrait of America

Chemicals, Cows, and Coal

The land of Tennessee is rich. There are just no two ways about it. The soil of the farmlands is fertile. The minerals are plentiful. The forests are beautiful and full of wildlife. People who are born in Tennessee don't usually want to leave.

And these days, most of them don't have to. Industry is thriving. Nashville, the capital of the state, is called "The Country Music Capital of the World," "The Religious Publishing Capital of the World," "The Wall Street of the South," and so on and so forth. After a rough economic history, Tennessee is coming into its own.

Manufacturing is big in this southern state. It accounts for about 85 percent of the value of goods produced here and

A farm in the Sequatchie Valley.

ances, motors, and generators. And there are dozens of other, smaller industries. Altogether, Tennessee's plants and factories manufacture about $14 billion worth of goods each year.

Agriculture, though smaller, is an important part of life in Tennessee. Half of the state is covered by farmland. And agriculture accounts for about 11 percent of the value of goods produced, about $1.75 billion worth.

More than half of that comes from livestock. Tennessee farmers raise beef cattle, dairy cattle,

employs almost 30 percent of the work force.

The people of Tennessee work in chemical plants that manufacture paints, plastic, medicine and soap. They make chemicals for farms and for industry.

In Chattanooga and Memphis, there are huge stockyards where cattle from around the state are brought to market. In these and other cities, there are meat-packing plants where beef and hogs are processed.

Also in Chattanooga and Memphis, there are factories that produce farm machinery, machinery for industry, and heating and refrigeration equipment. Around the state, Tennessee's workers make electrical equipment such as household appli-

The worker in a chemical plant (above) is contrasted with two of Tennessee's agricultural products . . . tobacco (right) and the famous Tennessee Walking Horse (far right).

and hogs. They also raise chickens for meat and for eggs.

The most glamorous Tennessee farm product is probably the Tennessee Walking Horse, raised in the Nashville Basin.

Tennessee's three largest cash crops are soybeans, tobacco, and corn. Most of the corn is grown for livestock feed. Cotton, a traditional southern crop, is still important in this state. Tennessee is a leader in cotton production.

Tennessee's farmers also grow truck crops, vegetables that are sold at market.

State of Tennessee Photographic Services

Harold W.T. Twitty

Here are two of Tennessee's popular tourist attractions. At the right is a section of the Memphis Pink Palace Museum, which features the region's natural and cultural history. Below, two children are playing in a pond on Mud Island, a theme park, near downtown Memphis, that presents the history of the Mississippi River.

In parts of Tennessee, mining is an important industry. It accounts for about 4 percent of the value of goods produced in the state. Coal is the most valuable mineral. Stone comes in second and zinc third.

Both farming and mining provide raw materials for the state's manufacturing.

Another of Tennessee's natural resources is its great beauty. Millions of tourists come to the state every year to wander through the Great Smoky Mountains National Park, a stretch of land in the Great Smoky Mountains that was bought from its private owners by the people of Tennessee and given to the nation as a park. They come to follow the Natchez Trace or visit the sites of great Civil War battles. They come for the dozens of arts and music festivals in the mountains. Or they come to the Grand Ole Opry. These tourists bring about $2.3 billion into Tennessee's economy each year.

Industry of all kinds is bringing prosperity to Tennessee . . . and changes to the lives of its people.

In addition to conventional attractions, tourists come to Tennessee for the calm beauty of the land.

State of Tennessee Photographic Services

Making the Cars

"Some people think I'm big in Detroit City.

From the letters that I write, they think I'm fine."

That country song spoke to a lot of people in Tennessee. Thousands of them had moved, over the years, to work in the factories of the North, making cars, only to discover that they had given up too much in exchange for a paycheck. Gary Montgomery thought about it.

"I always wanted to work in an automotive plant because of the pay, also because of the benefits. And I'd see it on TV and I'd say, 'Hey, you know, that's really neat. You know, I'd like to work there.' But I wasn't willing to move. I wanted to stay in the community that I grew up in...."

A few years ago, Gary Montgomery got the chance to have it both ways. The Japanese manufacturer, Nissan, decided to build a plant in Smyrna, Tennessee. They would be making compact sports trucks. But not everyone was as happy about it as Gary Montgomery.

"You had people that got a little bit negative—not knowing what to expect. They knew that the growth was going to take place. They wondered whether the advantages would outweigh the disadvantages. There were comments made such as, 'Hey, Smyrna may become a little Detroit or a little Tokyo.'"

And then 100,000 people applied for the first jobs. Some of them were Smyrna people. Some of them were from other automotive centers like Detroit. Now, 1,900 people are employed by the Nissan factory. They turn out 10,000 trucks every month.

"The native Tennesseeans have had a lot of pride within themselves and when they brought this company to the south, a lot of people said it couldn't be done. And even the Japanese themselves said, 'Hey, the Americans can't work, you know, like the Japanese.' And we were bound and determined to prove to the whole world that we could even build a better truck than what they're building in Japan. And all the statistics that have come out, all the reports, prove that to be a fact...."

And why not? The people of Tennessee have always shown that they could work as hard, and as well, as they play.

At the right is Gary Montgomery and an assembly line at the Nissan plant (above).

Homemade in Tennessee

There is a tradition in Tennessee of making fine things, at home, from the materials at hand. There are quilts made from the contents of a scrap basket. There are small wooden toys and carvings made from the trees of the forests. There are banjos made from ham cans and dulcimers played with feathers.

The artists of Tennessee follow in that tradition, making music and literature from the lives of the people.

A handful of examples.

George Washington Harris was a river boat pilot and a storyteller. His earthy tales were much admired by Mark Twain. They were collected in 1867, two years before his death, in a book called *Sut Lovingood: Yarns Spun by a Nat'ral Born*

Tennessee is known for its homemade quilts, which are often sold at the homes of the quilt makers.

Fool. Today, many critics believe he was the forerunner of such writers as Erskine Caldwell and William Faulkner, with his unsentimental stories of life among the South's poor whites.

W.C. Handy created his music out of the blues sung by blacks in the South. Born in Alabama, he came to Memphis in 1905, formed a band, and began to compose and perform the music that would make him famous. His "St. Louis Blues" sold more records at that time than any other single piece of music. Handy was the first person to put down on paper many of the traditional blues songs of his culture.

Roark Bradford, a white man, wrote stories based on black culture. His book, *Ol' Man Adam and His Chillun,* was adapted by Marc Connelly into the long-running Broadway hit, *Green Pastures.*

Against the background of the famous Beale Street in Memphis is W.C. Handy (left).

Memphis/Shelby County Public Library and Information Center

James Agee.

James Agee first came to the attention of the world with the book, *Let Us Now Praise Famous Men,* about Southern sharecroppers. He wrote the words, Walker Evans provided the photographs. Later, in 1958, his novel, *A Death in the Family,* won the Pulitzer Prize, and the play based on it, *All the Way Home,* won the prize in 1961. Agee also wrote many screenplays for films. His best work was based on life in the Tennessee he grew up in.

And of course, it is not possible to talk about the culture of Tennessee without mentioning the down home country music.

Sweet Country Music

"Diane, this is an old fiddle tune that I want you to learn to play. It's called 'Did You Ever See the Devil, Uncle Joe?' . . . I learned it from an old fiddle player when I was your age. And I want you to listen to me play it. I want you to learn to play it. And I want to hear you play it."

At the Smithville Jamboree, fiddler Frazier Moss passes on

Three scenes from the Smithville Jamboree.

an old tune to a young fiddler. That scene has been repeated in these mountains for generations. Just as the people of Tennessee made their own clothes and tools, they made their own music. And they still make it, in Smithville and in Nashville.

"I knew that I was addicted to music. I knew that I loved it and every time I heard a new song it excited me. I think it wasn't till I was in tenth grade of high school . . . I performed in front of my school at the talent show and I won it. I got real excited . . . so it wasn't till then that I decided I really wanted to start doing it."

Wynonna Judd's mother Naomi didn't let her try to make it in the big time until she finished high school. But after Wynonna's graduation, both of them started working on the dream. They started singing together, using the close harmonies of traditional Tennessee music. And they started looking for a break.

"During the last five years, I supported the two kids and myself making a living as a registered nurse in the Williamson County Hospital down where we lived. I was taking care of a young girl whose father was one of Nashville's top producers, Brent Maher. I became satisfied that he was the man. So on my day off from the hospital, I put my best dress on and went in and took him a tape."

The rest, as they say, is history. Brent Maher worked with the Judds and produced their first record, "Mama, He's Crazy."

They made a music video, an album, another hit.

And while the hits keep rolling out of Nashville, the music keeps rolling out of the hills of Tennessee. The banjo players and fiddlers keep playing. And the music is passed on for another generation.

"That's fine, Diane. You've done a fine job. Just think about that. That's the first time she ever heard it. I'm proud of this girl."

Naomi and Wynonna Judd.

Tomorrow's Tennessee

"**W**hat is America's oldest, continuously running radio show?" If you asked that question in a trivia game, the chances are good that half the people playing—even if they weren't country music fans—could answer. The Grand Ole Opry. To see how Tennessee has moved and is moving from yesterday to tomorrow, this Tennessee tradition might be a good place to start.

It began with a small radio show in 1925. The music was country—bluegrass, mountain music, cowboy blues. Over the years, the red brick Ryman Auditorium became a place that country singers and fans dreamed about. If you made it to the Opry, you'd made it.

Today, there's Opryland, U.S.A., a huge theme park on

A performance at Opryland.

Nashville . . . one example of the Tennessee tradition of the new becoming part of the old.

the outskirts of Nashville. There's the Country Music Hall of Fame. The show is broadcast from a bright new auditorium. But people all over the country still tune in on Saturday night to hear the old singers and the new ones, the comedians who have become part of the family, the commercials for candy bars— the Opry.

That's Tennessee. It's a place where people are not afraid of the future, of progress, of new industry. At the same time, it's a place where traditions are valued. The old is not replaced, it becomes part of the new.

Perhaps that attitude comes from a time-honored practice of not throwing things away. Whatever you had, in the days of the early settlers, you found a use for. You couldn't afford to waste things, so you found value in just about everything.

As Tennessee moves into the future, this quality is standing it in good stead.

Important Historical Events in Tennessee

1540 Spanish explorer Hernando de Soto leads an expedition into the Tennessee River Valley.

1541 De Soto reaches the Mississippi River and camps near what is now Memphis.

1665 Tennessee is included in a charter given to the Carolina Company of England.

1673 Two English explorers, James Needham and Gabriel Arthur, travel through the Tennessee River Valley. Louis Joliet and Jacques Marquette also explore the Tennessee region.

1682 Robert Cavelier, Sieur de la Salle, claims the Mississippi River Valley for France.

1714 A trading post is established by Charles Charleville at French Lick, near Nashville.

1760 Daniel Boone explores the eastern part of Tennessee.

1763 The Treaty of Paris is signed ending the French and Indian War. Under the terms of the treaty, France gives up its land east of the Mississippi to Great Britain.

1769 The first permanent white settler, William Bean of Virginia, builds a house near the Watauga River.

1772 Settlers in the Tennessee wilderness set up an independent government and write one of the first constitutions in North America. It is called the Watauga Association.

1775 The Transylvania Land Company buys large amounts of land from the Cherokee Indians, including Tennessee and Kentucky. Daniel Boone blazes the Wilderness Trail.

1777 Jonesboro is the first chartered town in Tennessee.

1780 James Robertson and John Donelson lead groups of settlers into the Tennessee wilderness around the Big Salt Lick and build Fort Nashborough on the Cumberland River. These settlers sign a governmental agreement called the Cumberland Compact.

1784 Three counties in eastern Tennessee rebel against North Carolina and create their own State of Franklin.

1794 Blount College (the University of Tennessee) is founded at Knoxville.

1796 Tennessee becomes the 16th state on June 1. The capital is Knoxville, and the governor is John Sevier.

1813 The war with the Creek Indians is begun by General Andrew Jackson.

1818 The United States buys land east of the Mississippi River from the Chickasaw Indians. This includes western Tennessee.

1829 Andrew Jackson of Tennessee becomes the seventh president of the United States.

1838 The Cherokee Indians are forced out of Tennessee.

1843 The state capital is moved to Nashville.

1845 James K. Polk from Columbia becomes the eleventh president of the United States.

1865 An amendment to the state constitution frees slaves. Andrew Johnson becomes the seventeenth president of the United States after President Lincoln is assassinated.

1866 Tennessee becomes the first Confederate state to be readmitted to the Union.

1870 Tennessee adopts a new state constitution.

1878 About one-quarter of the population of Memphis is wiped out by a yellow fever epidemic. Memphis loses its city charter after the disaster and does not regain it until 1893.

1925 John Scopes is convicted of teaching evolution in the public schools.

1933 The Tennessee Valley Authority is created by Congress.

1942 The Oak Ridge atomic energy plant is built by the federal government.

1953 Voters in Tennessee adopt eight new amendments to the state constitution.

1968 Civil rights leader Martin Luther King, Jr., is assassinated in Memphis.

1974 The state passes a law allowing the public to attend local and state governmental meetings.

Tennessee Almanac

Nickname. The Volunteer State.

Capital. Nashville.

State Bird. Mockingbird.

State Flower. Iris.

State Tree. Tulip poplar.

State Motto. Agriculture and Commerce.

State Song. The Tennessee Waltz.

State Abbreviations. Tenn. (traditional); TN (postal).

Statehood. June 1, 1796, the 16th state.

Government. Congress: U.S. senators, 2; U.S. representatives, 9. **State Legislature:** senators, 33; representatives, 99. **Counties:** 95.

Area. 42,244 sq. mi. (109,411 sq. km.), 34th in size among the states.

Greatest Distances. north/south, 115 mi. (185 km.); east/west, 480 mi. (772 km.).

Elevation. Highest: Clingmans Dome, 6,643 ft. (2,025 m). **Lowest:** 182 ft. (55 m).

Population. 1980 Census: 4,590,750 (17% increase over 1970), 17th among the states. **Density:** 109 persons per sq. mi. (42 persons per sq. km.). **Distribution:** 60% urban, 40% rural. **1970 Census:** 3,926,018.

Economy. Agriculture: soybeans, tobacco, wheat, cotton, corn, beef cattle, hogs and pigs. **Manufacturing:** chemicals, food products, electric and electronic equipment, nonelectric machinery, fabricated metal products, rubber and plastics products. **Mining:** coal, zinc, stone.

Places to Visit

Andrew Johnson National Historic Site in Greenville.

American Museum of Atomic Energy in Oak Ridge.

Blount Mansion in Knoxville.

Grand Ole Opry House, near Nashville.

Great Smoky Mountains National Park.

Lookout Mountain, near Chattanooga.

The Hermitage, near Nashville.

The Parthenon in Nashville.

Annual Events

Wildflower Pilgrimage in Gatlinburg (April).

World's Biggest Fish Fry in Paris (April).

Cotton Carnival in Memphis (May).

Iroquois Steeplechase in Nashville (May).

Annual Tennessee Bluegrass Festival in Cosby (June).

Nashville's Country Music Fanfare (June).

Tennessee State Fair in Nashville (September).

Liberty Bowl Football Game in Memphis (December).

Tennessee Counties

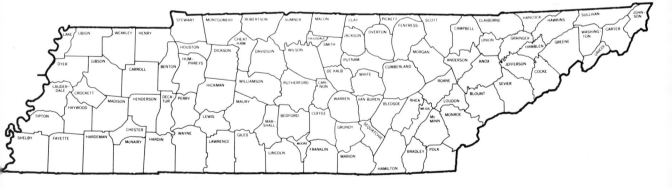

© American Map Corporation
License 18920